PROVERBIAL SUCCESS

**Your No Nonsense Daily Success Guide
based on the book of Proverbs**

Scotty V. Jones

© 2014 Scotty V. Jones
Gr8 Day Media LLC

Table of Contents

Introduction

Stephen K. Scott was failure at most everything. For the first six years out of college, he got fired from every job he had. His best friend then challenged him to study a chapter in the book of Proverbs each day for one year and by doing so, promised that he would experience success and happiness beyond what he had ever known.

Stephen took his friend up on that challenge, and today is billionaire.

The book of Proverbs was written to give "prudence to the simple, knowledge and discretion to the young" (1:4), and to make the wise even wiser (1:5)

Proverbs is based upon the wisdom of King Solomon who, was believed to be one of the wisest men on his time. However, his wisdom wasn't the only wealth he possessed. His gold reserves would be worth over a trillion dollars in today's dollars. This is why I feel that Proverbs is a definite go to book on the subject of wealth and success and why I wrote this book.

It's a simple to read, short book that teaches you often overlooked wisdom strategies for achieving breakthrough success in health, marriage, work and most importantly, a relationship with God.

With this book, I hope to offer you some of the same invaluable lessons that I've learned which have helped me to reach the top of 3 different companies in my field as well as becoming a successful author and entrepreneur with numerous successful companies.

There are 31 chapters in the book of Proverbs so you should be able to easily read a chapter a day. I recommend you study a chapter daily with your bible to get the best results from your future efforts.

At the end of a year, if you study a chapter each day, you will have read the book of Proverbs 12 times. I challenge you to do so as I have and I can promise you that your life will be blessed beyond measure. Success and happiness will be yours!

Enjoy the book!

Scotty V. Jones

Chapter 1 - Success Lesson #1: Why Proverbs?

Proverbs tells you right away the purpose of this book. The aim of the entire book of Proverbs is listed in the following verses.

Verse 2 tells you that Proverbs will teach how to recognize wisdom and instruction (in the Hebrew the word is discipline, which we also need).

Wisdom is not only having information about something, but applying it at the right time.

This will take understanding of the circumstance, which Proverbs does by writing it like a parable (a short story to teach you something).

Verse 3 shows you that you have to be deliberate on receiving the instruction ("to receive").

Receive means *to take*. It's on purpose. We have to, on purpose, choose to take the

instruction we need in order to have the
wisdom

Verse 4 shows you who this is for: the
simple. That is to say, someone who just is
what he or she is.

In other words, it's someone who "keeps it
real, doesn't over complicate things."

If you are ready to live a life of health,
wealth, and happiness, then studying
Proverbs will be the perfect guide for you.
Stay open to God's direction in your life.

Tomorrow's lesson: The missing link to
your success...

Chapter 2 - Success Lesson #2: The Missing Link

Today's power verse comes from **Proverbs 2 verse 7**:

"He grants a treasure of common sense to the honest. He is a shield to those who walk in integrity". (NLT)

My pastor was speaking at a conference not to long ago, and he was teaching about the five senses. He made a comment that sounded funny when he said it:

"Everyone can develop his or her sixth sense. Most are just not operating in it".

That sixth sense... is **COMMON SENSE**!

At first I wasn't sure why it was called "common" sense if many people don't walk in it. However, I've come to find out as you begin to yield to the wisdom in Proverbs that you begin to see its simplicity.

So maybe the missing link **_IS_** common sense, it's just not functioning in your life because you aren't yielding to it.

You know it in your head but it hasn't really become part of your conscious mind has it?

As you study out the book of Proverbs, allow its wisdom to become second nature to you. Over time you will see how it gives you power through it's simple messages, thus, giving you the keys to success in your day to day life.

This is why reading it over and over is so important. It's **imperative** to meditate on it day and night. Pretty soon, the principles will become common sense to you.

Tomorrow's lesson: The Favor Factor

Chapter 3 - Success Lesson #3: The Favor Factor

Verses 3 and 4 of Proverbs 3 are today's power verses:

"Never let loyalty and kindness leave you! Tie them around your neck as a reminder. Write them deep within your heart. Then you will find favor with both God and people, and you will earn a good reputation." (NLT)

What is favor and why should we want it?

The free dictionary defines it as **"A gracious, friendly, or obliging act that is freely given."** It can also mean "a privilege or concession". Freely given in this context are the key words.

It is God's favor that opens up doors for us. His goodness causes even strangers to show us generosity at times. Notice that it tells you to tie it around your neck if you have to!

Writing them deep within your heart means you have to make a conscience effort to make this part of your life.

Proverbs 1:2 reflects a bit on meditation. Meditation is a key to success in anything. One definition of meditation is repeating prayers to yourself over and over again.

Here is a quick daily prayer that I use to continue to receive God's favor:

"Thank you Father that I have favor with you, and you have given me favor with man, and it goes before me everywhere that I go in Jesus name." AMEN.

So what is the <u>secret</u> to continually flow in God's favor?

It's found in Verse 3: **Loyalty and kindness.**

Tap into the favor factor today. When we do our part, God will do His.

You've just been shown one way to begin
implementing what you are
learning. Remember to keep it simple!

Tomorrow's lesson: Nothing to hold you
back

Chapter 4 - Success Lesson #4: Nothing to hold you back

Today's power verse is found in **Verse 12 of Proverbs 4**:

"When you walk, you won't be held back; when you run, you won't stumble."(NLT)

Have you ever experienced a time when it seems you are taking two steps forward, but fall three steps back?

No matter what you seem to do, you just can't get ahead. It might be your job, your finances, your health, or your relationships.

If you've ever been in that season before or you are there now, **there is hope!**

Wisdom is applicable knowledge. Thinking back to a bad decision you've made, after some time you probably realized a few things that became crystal clear didn't you?

You were missing knowledge that, had you received it at the time, you would have decided differently.

There are three things that work together:

Knowledge (what), **Understanding (why)**, and **Wisdom (application)**.

As you are reading your daily chapter in Proverbs, remember this is your daily dose of Knowledge.

Writing your personal notes in a journal will help you remember what you have been reading so you can refer to it right when you need it.

You'll soon see that as you walk in the ways of wisdom, you will **no longer** be held back or stumble.

Nothing in this world can hold you back from your destiny but you!

Tomorrow's Lesson: Sexual Purity

Chapter 5 - Success Lesson #5: Sexual Purity

Today's power verse comes
from **Proverbs 10:5:**

*"And strange men may be full of your
wealth, and the fruit of your work go to the
house of others."* (Bible in Basic English
Translation)

The subject to this verse is also found in the
previous verses: **The warnings of getting
mixed up in sexual immorality.**

The name of this translation fits here.
Proverbs can't get any clearer than this:

**Get mixed up in sexual immorality and
you are subject to have all your wealth
taken away. Not only will that be
taken away, everything you built will be
given to another.**

This isn't only speaking about wealth. There
is more to life than wealth, like a legacy.
You can work all your life and build
something great to last, only to lose it all in

an instant for not protecting yourself against sexual immorality.

No one is immune. But everyone can protect themselves.

Do you know why Billy Graham never had a sex scandal? Why? Simply, because he refused to be alone with a woman that wasn't related to him. If he counseled them, there was at least one other person present.

On his crusades, if his wife wasn't with him, he would have someone go into the hotel room before he walked in to "sweep the place" and make sure that no one was there.

It might seem extreme to you, but we should follow the legacy of a great man of God that remained pure when others could not.

It's okay to be a little extreme when it comes to protecting yourself and your relationships. They are yours to take care of, so choose wisely!

Tomorrow's lesson: Deliver Yourself

Chapter 6 - Success Lesson #6: Deliver Yourself

Today's power verse is found in **Verse 3 from Proverbs 6**:

"Do this now, my son, and deliver thyself, when thou art come into the hand of thy friend; go, humble thyself, and make sure thy friend".

In **Verse 3,** Proverbs tells you that you can be **snared** by the words of your mouth.

How true is this, you could have avoided trouble only if you were more aware of what was spewing out from right under your nose?

So what should you do if your words snare you?

Deliver yourself (Set yourself free). Let me explain briefly...

God, our father, is gracious. He has already provided **EVERYTHING** you need in order for you to be successful.

Even when you miss the opportunity, He
has already planned a way out for you. And
in this instance, He expects you to do it
yourself.

YOU are in control of your lips. He's not
going to control them for you. He
will **empower** you, but you will need to
create what you want with them. He will
back you up.

So when you stumble and your words
snare you, deliver yourself. **Don't let pride
control you!**

Humble yourself and expect mercy and
grace to cover you. Allow the wisdom that
you have been learning to come up from
inside you and take over.

In times of conflict, **agree quickly with the
one that is upset and speak softly to turn
away wrath.** These things seem so simple
until you actually have to do it.

But once you do it, you will see the success
and it will build the confidence you need, so
when it happens again, you will immediately

put into action what you've learned and you
will achieve that desired outcome you seek.

Tomorrow's lesson: Power in Your Midst

Chapter 7 - Success Lesson #7: Power in your midst

Today's power verse comes from **Proverbs 7 and Verse 21**:

"With her much fair speech she caused him to yield, with the flattering of her lips she forced him".

Solomon, despite all his wisdom, ended up making some of the dumbest choices one can make. In the end, he turned it around, but it cost him his life.

The power of speech is one of the strongest themes in Proverbs.

Genesis shows us the power of words filled with perfect faith: *it manifests when spoken rapidly*. We are created in God's image and likeness. We are created to function like Him.

Because of that truth, **you have the power
to create or to destroy with the words of
your mouth!**

Proverbs teaches that there is power in
sincere praise. It also explains the
destruction gossip creates, not only for the
listener, but also the speaker and the one
being spoken about. And here we are
reminded that the power of our speech can
cause someone to yield to do something
they wouldn't normally do.

We will be held accountable for everything
we say. **Matthew 12:36 from the
NASB** states:

*"But I tell you that every careless word that
people speak, they shall give an accounting
for it in the Day of Judgment"*.

The "Day of Judgment" doesn't necessarily
mean *"The Day"*, but when the fruit of the
words you've spoken come to life.

Your homework assignment: Think of all
the times in the past when you where either
directly or indirectly involved with
gossip. What was the outcome for all?

In your *"Day"*, what can be said about
some of the words you've spoken?

Tomorrow's lesson: God's ways of
increase

Chapter 8 - Success Lesson #8: God's Ways of Increase

Today's power verse comes from **Verse 21 of Proverbs 8**:

"That I may cause those that love me to inherit substance; and I will fill their treasures"

In this chapter, **wisdom is personified in Verses 1-11.**

Verses 12-21 give us the benefits of receiving wisdom into our lives. One of those is **substance**.

Verse 21 blows away the theory that God wants you to be poor!

It makes no difference to God if you want to be poor. But if you don't want to be poor, He has provided a way for you to be filled with treasures.

There are rules that are set up in order for you to have increase. You can do it God's way, for with God's way He adds no sorrow with it. Or you can do it the world's way, and what God doesn't establish He isn't under obligation to protect.

In **Matthew 6:33,** God tells you that when you put His Kingdom first, His way of doing and being right, all you need will be added unto you. It will be added. You don't have to go after it and toil for it.

This doesn't mean that you don't work for it. **You still work**. But the working will not be one of toiling. **You won't have to work two jobs just to make ends meet.**

When you put God first and honor Him in this way, He will open up opportunities for you to increase. He'll multiply the little you have in your hand. It goes back to the compounded interest.

Because you took the time to invest in God's economy (His way of doing and being right), He makes sure that your dividends are plenty. God is a good God and wants you to have the best.

You should expect it and allow God to lead the way.

Tomorrow's lesson: It's Time to Live!

Chapter 9 - Success Lesson # 9: It's Time to Live

Today's power verse can be found in **Verse 6 of Proverbs 9**:

"Forsake the foolish, and live; and go in the way of understanding."

When God told Abraham to leave all he knew in **Genesis 12** and go to a place that He would show him, many thought that Abraham was the foolish one.

But sometimes you need to look like the fool, even when you aren't, so that you may live! And sometimes that means moving away from all you know.

The Hebrew word for life **"chayah"** is a verb meaning to have continued life and live prosperously. It means to be made alive, be quickened, restored to life or health.

This is the kind of life God wants you to have. But in order to have this kind of life,

you need to do your part and forsake
foolish things.

When God gives you instructions, it will
seem foolish to you at times because it will
be in contradiction of what you have been
taught. In God's economy, you give to get.
You don't toil, because all has been
provided already through the sacrifice of
Jesus.

When someone cuts you off in traffic, you
love them anyway.

What was Abraham's reward for going the
way of understanding? He ended up not
only having one son, but that through that
lineage the Messiah would be born! There's
always a reward from God that is much
more than we can ask or think.

It's worth going the way of understanding
and leaving behind those things that, in the
end, will only hinder what you were created
to do.

Tomorrow's lesson: Lay up now,
Withdraw later

**Chapter 10 - Success Lesson #10: Lay up
now, Withdraw later**

Today's power verse can be found in **Verse
14 of Proverbs 10**:

*"Wise [men] lay up knowledge: but the
mouth of the foolish [is] near destruction."*

**This is one of the secrets that come out
from Proverbs as you carefully study it.**

You need to purposefully lay things up that
you need. Just as the ant diligently works
without a taskmaster, but stores up for
when the food is needed, so must you also
lay up the knowledge to draw from when
you need it.

It is so important to go through the daily
exercise of writing down something
pertaining to today.

You might not realize it now, but what you
are doing is laying up the knowledge you
will need later. While engaging your soul in
these lessons (your mind, will, and

emotions), you will have a better chance of remembering what you are reading.

There will come a time when the seed is dormant that after your reading life will spring up. It will be a time when a situation comes up out of nowhere.

Perhaps someone comes up to you angrily and you now know to stay calm and give a soft answer. Or perhaps a business opportunity comes up.

You now know what three characteristics are in a wicked person so you wouldn't want to do business with that person.

As you continue the journey through Proverbs, you will be surprised on how easily your language will begin to change. Instead of words that can cause ruin like a foolish person, your words will start to mirror the wisdom found in Proverbs.

Tomorrow's lesson: What's true humility?

Chapter 11 - Success Lesson #11: What Is True Humility

Thought of the day....

How difficult would it be to remain humble if someone wronged you?

Today's power verse can be found in **Verse 2 of Proverbs 11**:

"When pride cometh,then cometh shame: but with the lowly is wisdom".

Now before getting offended by the word "lowly" the word here actually means to be full of humility, to be humble.

You've heard the saying about pride, *"pride cometh before the fall"*. **It is often your pride that gets you into trouble in your actions.**

How many times have you done something wrong or said something wrong to someone and knew you were wrong but still couldn't bring yourself to apologize?

If you're honest with yourself, it would be more times than you can count. But the lesson here is simple, if you are to succeed in business, succeed in life, succeed in anything, you **MUST** first learn to be humble.

- That means listening to the counsel of others that have achieved the level of success you are seeking.
- It means listening and looking for opportunities that may not always come wrapped with a bow and a guarantee.
- You may have to cross a bridge or two you have burned and repair a broken friendship or relationship....

However this rule applies in your life, it is up to you to take on the mindset of this scripture and become "*lowly*".

Perhaps all the blessings that have been just missing you, will finally start to manifest themselves once you practice a bit of humility....

Tomorrow's lesson: The Power of Words

**Chapter 12 - Success Lesson #12: The
Power of Words**

Today's power verse is found in **Verse 18
of Chapter 12**:

*"Careless words stab like a sword, but the
words of wise people bring healing."* (God's
Word Translation)

According to the Hebrew, **the word The
King James uses as piercing also is
translated as stab.**

It looks like on this one, God's Word
translation gives you a clearer picture of
what you do when you lie, gossip, or speak
wickedly (in other words anything God
doesn't say or do).

Most people normally don't think that their
words have such an effect, but **Chapter 12
of Proverbs** is full of revealing the power of
your words, for your well being or your
destruction.

On the flip side, God shows you that just as
you can easily stab with your words, you
can also bring healing with them.

Have you ever been down and had a friend
tell you something that just broke through
all the depression and hurt which either
made you laugh or just caused you to see
the light again?

How powerful are our words!

Choose your words wisely!!!

The power of words are even demonstrated
in science. Dr. Masuro Emoto wrote an
interesting book called **"The Hidden
Messages in Water"**.

In this book, he demonstrates what
happens to filtered water when negative
words are spoken into it instead of positive
ones.

If you would like to learn more about the
power of your words, Dr. Emoto's book is
an interesting one to add to your library.

Tomorrow's lesson: Poor Rich Man

Chapter 13 - Success Lesson #13: Poor Rich Man

Today's power verse is found in **Verse 7 of Chapter 13**:

"There is he that maketh himself rich, yet [hath] nothing: [there is] he that maketh himself poor, yet [hath] great riches."

For the rich man (not all rich men), he is indeed poor when he lives in gratitude to what God has provided for him and lives a life without the grace of God.

For what benefit would all the riches in the world give him when it cannot buy him into the gates of heaven?

Fear causes the rich man to live out injustice and be uncharitable.

For the poor man (not all poor men), he is indeed rich, and yet fails to recognize that God is the same yesterday, today, and forever (Hebrews 13:8).

He is our Sheppard who promises we shall
not lack **(Psalm 23:1)**, and yet the poor
man pretends to be wealthy if only for the
honor that it might bestow him.

What the poor man doesn't understand is
that he already has all that he needs
because the Father has provided. <u>**All you
need to do is ask for it**</u>.

Notice the verse says that there is one that
makes himself either rich or poor when one
isn't.

Both, ironically, have the same root causing
them to live in such hypocrisy: **FEAR!**

Both are caused by failing to see God as
He truly is.

Examine yourself today. How do you see
God? Don't pretend. Be honest with
yourself and Him and be set free.

<u>Tomorrow's lesson:</u> Watch Your Step

Chapter 14 - Success Lesson #14: Watch Your Step

Today's power verse comes from **Verse 14 of Chapter 15**:

"A gullible person believes anything, but a sensible person watches his step." (God's Word Translation)

It is an unfortunate by-product in the fall of Adam that you cannot instantly trust with 100% certainty what someone tells you.

We all have a very trusting nature and have learned the hard way not to be so gullible.

You can see the best in everyone, which also has opened the door to being hurt (emotionally).

You've behaved foolishly, believing anything someone would tell you (not so much of anything negative about a person, but of what, perhaps what they were going to do).

The assumption was because you behave in a certain way, then others do to. That is just not the case. Although you should not instantly believe the worst, it is wisest to *"try before you trust"*.

"We are to prove all things and believe not every spirit" **(1 Thessalonians 5:21 and 1 John 4:1)**.

Depend on God's Holy Spirit to reveal to you what you need to know.

Trusting God to direct your steps is one way to ensure you don't fall into the trap of being foolish.

But if you do fall into the trap, be quick to forgive. Forgive not only the one who fooled you, but also yourself.

Do not allow the actions of others to harden your heart. You can't help what others do, but you can control what your reactions are toward them.

<u>**Tomorrow's lesson:**</u> Getting Answers to Prayers

**Chapter 15 - Success Lesson #15:
Getting Answers to Prayers**

Today's power verse comes from **Verse 8
of Proverbs 15**:

*"A sacrifice brought by wicked people is
disgusting to the LORD, but the prayers of
decent people please him."* (Gods Word in
Translation)

**Decent people, as translated in the GWT,
are what the KJV calls *"THE UPRIGHT"*.**

It's from the Hebrew word *"yashar"*,
meaning just.

*A just person is one who has received the
gift of righteousness through Jesus
Christ* **(John 14:6)**.

Because you have decided that God's
sacrifice was enough, God is pleased to
hear your prayers.

So why is the sacrifice of the wicked
disgusting?

Because the sacrifices are made without any regard to who God really is.

It is coming to God on their terms, not by the terms that God has set forth in his word.

It is stating that the blood of Jesus was not enough and that something needed to be added.

If you want to have your prayers answered, check to see what your actions are telling God.

Do you believe that the blood of Jesus was enough for Him to hear you?

Receive the revelation that the blood is enough. It's enough because God loves you and provided a way to always hear you when you cry out to Him.

The only thing you are adding is faith that he is who he says he is and he will do what he says he will do.

Tomorrow's lesson: Succeeding in Everything

**Chapter 16 - Success Lesson #16:
Succeeding in Everything**

Today's power verse comes from **Verse 3 of Proverbs 16**:

*"Commit to the **LORD** whatever you do, and your plans will succeed".(NLT)*

The Hebrew word for translated is *"machashabah"* or *"machashebeth"*, both meaning "**thoughts, devices, plans, purposes, invention**" according to Lexicon.

God wants all your thoughts, devices, plans, purposes, and inventions to succeed--to prosper. It's to be settled, it's a done deal.

Commit in the Hebrew is the word **"galal"**.

Most of the definitions have to do with rolling something. So what is God telling you here?

In order for your thoughts, devices, plans, purposes, and inventions to

**continually succeed, you need to roll
away what you are doing to him.**

For instance, imagine playing catch with a
child.

When you roll your plans over to God; God
catches it; He returns it to you; you take
hold of it; so on and so forth.

The ball is continually in play because God
is making sure nothing is "mis-handled".
He's looking out for you because you have
chosen to engage him.

Do you want to succeed?

**Engage God in your plans today. He is
the God that can do it. He is the God that
will do it.**

You don't always know how, but that part is
irrelevant.

Tomorrow's lesson: There is time to turn
things around

Chapter 17 - Success Lesson #17: There IS Time to Turn Things Around

Today's power verse comes from **Verse 22 in Proverbs 17**:

"A merry heart doeth good like medicine; but a broken spirit drieth the bones".

God always wants you to keep a good attitude even when times are difficult.

It is during these times of strife that he wants you to be positive and even yes, HAPPY!

Because he wants the best for you, sometimes you have to be taught lessons in order to understand and appreciate the blessings given.

So the words above are true, there is time to turn things around no matter how dire things seem.

You should be encouraged after hearing these words because it should signify that your time is indeed coming, **God has blessings with your name on them!**

Even all those times when you did people
wrong, acted just plain evil; all those
actions can be turned around with a
cheerful spirit in the LORD!

Also remember the power of your words
and the damage they can do if negative; as
well as the healing they can provide when
used positively.

Each day we all make mistakes but God
gives the chance to redeem ourselves
through prayer and repentance.

**A new day is a new opportunity to
become what God has called you to be
regardless of where you were yesterday;
today is a new day and you should
rejoice!**

Tomorrow's lesson: Your life is in your
tongue

Chapter 18 - Success Lesson #18: Your Life Is In Your Tongue

Today's power verse comes from **Verse 21 in Proverbs 18:**

"Death and life are in the power of the tongue; and they that love it shall eat the fruit thereof."

Whatever results you have in life are a direct result of the words you speak. Whether positive or negative, you have a hand in making good things happen or bad things happen.

If you are one who constantly speaks negativity, doesn't it always seem like nothing ever quite works out for you?

And if you constantly speak in a positive manner, things may not always work out in your favor, but you always seem to take the good out of the situation, don't you?

God gives you the power to make decisions. YOU are the only life form he created that has this gift.

Animals rely on their natural instincts.
Plants rely on the weather, moon, etc.

You are truly blessed when you put things
into this context!

**Whatever you think and speak about the
most always manifests itself in your
life.** It also speaks in **Verse 6 about a
fool's mouth is his destruction**.

God is trying to teach you a valuable lesson
here; **you have the power to open your
mouth and speak freely about whatever
you want.**

But are you using that power he has given
you to inflict life or death, hope or despair?

**You must learn to speak positives into
existence when you talk, you must learn
to speak wisdom instead of speaking
ignorance, or spreading gossip.**

To be successful in anything, it takes a
positive attitude to be sure.

When you put God first and truly put the
principle of this lesson into action, watch

and see how things start to happen in a
mighty way for you.

Tomorrow's lesson: How not to ruin your
children

Chapter 19 - Success Lesson #19: How NOT to RUIN your children

Today's power verse comes from **Verse 18 of Proverbs 19**:

"Chasten thy son while there is hope, and let not thy soul spare for his crying".

For people with children, this should speak directly to your heart.

It encourages you that in order to really be a good parent, you will have to make sure to discipline them, even if it's hard work for you.

Observing the children around you, you know who are disciplined and who are not.

You may think you are doing your child a disservice if you don't give them what they want. You want them to "be happy."

What makes them happy today is not going to make them happy next month. They are children. They don't really know what real happiness is.

You want them to live a long, healthy, prosperous life.

If they would adhere to wisdom, then they will be happy.

But put the child's happiness over discipline because you as a parent, are too lazy or don't want to see the child sad, would be condemning that child to ruin.

While they are young is when there is hope. Discipline your children now so that they may live a prosperous life. Every child is different.

Ask God how you can discipline your child effectively. He created him/her. He knows best.

Think about this: If you have children, what is your best way to discipline them?

If you don't have any children but know people that do, why not pray that they receive wisdom on how to discipline them

correctly so that they grow up to be
prosperous adults?

Tomorrow's lesson: Seeing the
Opportunities Available...

Chapter 20 - Success Lesson #20:
Seeing the Opportunities Available

Today's power verse comes from **Verse 13 of Proverbs 20**:

"Love not sleep, lest thou come to poverty; open thine eyes, [and] thou shalt be satisfied with bread".

When we indulge in things like sleep we cannot then be surprised that we are without the simple necessities of life.

It is when we open our eyes to the opportunities of work that we will then be satisfied with what we need and want.

In God's system of doing things, there isn't such a thing as welfare. If you were hungry and were poor, you worked for what you got.

The farmers left the outskirts of their crops untouched so that the poor could glean (gather/harvest) food for themselves.

The church took care of the widows. The people, not the government, also took care of those with disabilities.

The systems like welfare in the United States were set up to help people.

Although I know many people who qualify for the assistance, I also know many that take advantage because in the end, they are lazy and do not want to work.

When we begin to understand that God is with us, it doesn't matter if we take a minimum wage job at a place like McDonald's.

We know that if we remain faithful (steady) and diligent, God will make sure we will increase.

If we would only trust Him to put into operation the Kingdom Principals He has set up we will not do without what we need.

He is faithful to His Word and in it He has set up promises of provision as we do things His way.

If you want something you've never had,
you will have to do something you've never
done.

Dare to believe what God tells you in His
Word. He will come through for you when
you allow Him to direct you.

What opportunities for increase are in your
path today? Start opening your eyes to the
opportunities God is placing in front of you
and watch how things change in a mighty
way!

Tomorrow's lesson: Completely
Satisfied...

**Chapter 21 - Success Lesson #21:
Completely Satisfied**

Today's power verses found in **Verse 21**:

*"He that followeth after righteousness and
mercy findeth life, righteousness, and
honor."*

This verse reminds me of **Matthew 5:6**. In
the Amplified translation it reads:

*"Blessed and fortunate and happy and
spiritually prosperous (in that state in which
the born again child of God enjoys His favor
and salvation) are those who hunger and
thirst for righteousness (uprightness and
right standing with God), for they shall be
completely satisfied."*

How many of us would like to be
completely satisfied?

Here, **in Proverbs**, it gives us the key. It is
the pursuit of both righteousness (right
standing with God) and mercy (unfailing
love). They are connected.

Righteousness, as we stated in a previous guide, is not something you can buy or earn. It is a free gift that God provides for you.

And even after you come to this realization and acceptance, it is this daily renewal of revelation of receiving the free gift that keeps your heart in the tender state of humility.

Because of the free gift of righteousness, it spurs you on to mercy.

Having a right standing with God opens you up to His way of thinking and doing.

One of God's attributes is being merciful. It is because of His unfailing loving kindness that He sent His son to pay the penalty of rebellion.

In the end, nothing is more satisfying than being God's friend and living out a life of acts of mercy.

Tomorrow's lesson: Need a raise? Try this...

Chapter 22 - Success Lesson #22: Need a raise? Try this!

Today's power verse is found in **Verse 29 of Proverbs 22**:

"Seest thou a man diligent in his business? he shall stand before kings; he shall not stand before mean [men]."

For several years now, I have continually received calls from head hunters seeking me out; even in a "down market". My secret is found in today's power text:

The King James calls it diligent. The NLT states this verse as: Do you see any truly competent workers? They will serve kings rather than working for ordinary people.

Diligence is described in the Word Reference online dictionary as **"quietly and steadily persevering especially in detail or exactness"**.

Diligence is something that first needs to be desired. Once you desire it, all you need is practice in that area.

It wasn't until I was in the marketplace that the lessons taught to me about diligence really started to sink in.

They reinforced my belief that if you are going to do something, you might as well do it right!

I've become a diligent people, which is why I am continually blessed.

Diligence **WILL** pay off for you to when you put it into practice.

But you must choose to do so. It's not just going to come upon you.

Choose to be diligent today and sooner or later the doors of blessing will open up wide to usher you into that promotion.

Tomorrow's lesson: The power of this one person in your life...

Chapter 23 - Success Lesson #23: The Power of this one person in your life

Today's power verse comes from **Verse 19**:

"Hear thou, my son, and be wise, and guide thine heart in the way."

The ministry of parenthood should not be taken lightly.

As a parent, you have a chance to be involved in the development of an extraordinary person.

As a parent, you have an unique opportunity to mold someone's future so that they can reach their full potential and fulfill their destiny.

The Hebrew word for hear in this verse is a verb that means not only to hear, but also to listen to and obey.

You can hear without truly listening and definitely not obeying.

Since we are made to follow our heart (spirit), it is important to protect it and feed it truth so that when decisions have to be made, the right ones will be chosen.

In order to make progress in your inner man (your heart) on your journey, you will need the benefit of a mentor.

That is basically what a parent is, a mentor. When we are older, we do not outgrow the need for a mentor.

A mentor is like a coach. It's the coach that wins games. And if you want to be all that you are destined to be, you will need a mentor too.

The great news is that there are many mentorship programs available.

Some people call it life coaching. But if you cannot afford one, God has One available to you, 24/7.

His name is the Holy Spirit and **He is available to mentor you in any area anytime you are ready.** Take advantage of His free offer today.

Tomorrow's lesson: How to earn over $340,000 without buying a home...

Chapter 24 - Success Lesson # 24: How to earn over $340,000 without buying a home

Today's power verse comes from **Verse 27 of Proverbs 24**:

"Prepare thy work without, and make it fit for thyself in the field; and afterwards build thine house".

Sometimes an opportunity comes to us to buy a home and when we look at our finances, we might believe we could afford to do so.

The problem with this is that not everything was thought through.

There are costs that you are not paying when you rent, such as:

- The cost of paying the taxes on the home;
- The cost of the light, gas, and water (which you don't pay now) will be higher than you are used to;
- The additional cost if something happened to your business or job

you will need at least six months of finances to help you through the lean times (that's good advice for anyone though);

- The cost of the upkeep of the home (just to name a few!).

Taking the figures from above, let's say you are increasing your costs by $500 a month. If you take that $500 a month and put it in a mutual fund (on average a mutual fund gives you a 12% return) and add $500 a month for 30 years (the length of a home loan) you will make $340, 259.12. Most homes do not give you that type of return.

You put in over $180,000.00 in 30 years by putting aside $500 a month. You made $160,259.12.

That is a return on your investment of about 47%. It's the beauty of compounded interest.

This does not include what you employer might be matching at your job in a 401K. This is just your part.

What about the increase of rent and things like that.

Well, if you are diligent in what you do, you will have increase to cover it and still invest in your future that $500 a month.

I'm not telling you not to purchase a home; neither is this verse.

What is just being highlighted here is that when you do want to buy a home, consider everything before making your decision.

If you don't own a home, would you now? If you do own a home, how can you pay it off faster so that you can then put the difference in investing further in your future?

Tomorrow's lesson: How to get a pay increase...

Chapter 25 - Success Lesson #25: How to get a pay increase

Today's power verse can be found in **Verse 13 of Chapter 25:**

"As the cold of snow in the time of harvest, [so is] a faithful messenger to them that send him: for he refresheth the soul of his masters."

The NLT is stated as Trustworthy messengers refresh like snow in summer. They revive the spirit of their employer.

It's interesting that Proverbs makes the connection between being a trustworthy employee to the welcoming of snow in the summer. It's refreshing and surprising.

In my observance and research, I've found it a shame that people are doing just enough at their jobs to not get fired.

Then these are the same people who complain when they barely get a cost of living increase at their review!

Their paycheck is seen as something that is owed to them out of obligation.

But did they not enter into an agreement to do the work for a certain amount of financial compensation?

How can one complain then if they aren't increased? What new problems have they solved?

How have they made things better? If one is doing exactly what they were hired to do, then one can expect to receive the same pay.

But, if you do a little more, what a refreshing thing that is to an employer! And worthy of increased compensation!

If you want a pay increase at your job, become refreshing to your boss!

Revive him/her by solving problems in your
department. You might be surprised
yourself with the outcome.

Tomorrow's lesson: The dainty morsels of
destruction...

Chapter 26 - Success Lesson #26: The Dainty Morsels of Destruction

Gossip...

Today's power verse is from the NLT, **Verse 22 of Proverbs 26**:

"Rumors are dainty morsels that sink deep into one's heart."

Rumors (gossip) are serious business.

You might not think that it's a big deal to spread news about another person's life, but in order to live a long, healthy, wealthy, whole life, this part of our daily lives must cease!

The trouble with gossip and why people repeat it is found in the first part of the verse: *they are dainty morsels*.

Dainty morsels are good to eat. You want more and more and more. Sounds kind of like gluttony, doesn't it? Didn't we just go over that in a previous chapter?

**Gossip is like gluttony of the soul.
Sooner or later, dis-ease (disease) sets
in.**

If you think that gossip doesn't affect you
because you only hear it and not repeat it,
think again.

This verse also exposes that to be false. It
affects your heart. And sooner or later,
when your heart (which is like a spiritual
container or a manufacturing center), is full,
it will come out.

And where does it come out from? It
overflows from your mouth. You eventually
repeat a matter, even if you didn't mean to.

You can stop the gossip by choosing not to
eat it.

Think about this.....

**Gossiping in the office is difficult to stop,
but not impossible. Refusing to partake
in it is a great start!**

Tomorrow's lesson: What's worse than
anger...

**Chapter 27 - Success Lesson #27:
What's worse than anger**

Today's power verse can be found in **Verse
4 of Proverbs 27:**

*"Wrath is cruel, and anger is outrageous;
but who is able to stand before envy?"*

Wrath does not only weigh heavily on the
person committing it, but also on the
person(s) it's being committed to.

**It's best to get out of the way when
someone is "on the war path" so that the
mischief they are drawing to themselves
will not also land on you.**

Anger here in proverbs is mentioned as
being outrageous. The Hebrew word for
this is: *sheteph*. Sheteph means: "flood,
downpour".

**Anger opens up floodgates you don't
want open! It can open up the doors to
sickness, disease, and even death.**

Envy is the worse of the three.

Jealousy kicked Lucifer out of heaven, taking down with him one third of the celestial hosts. Jealously in his heart to be like God led to pride, which led to his, well, dismissal.

It was jealously that caused Cain to kill his brother, Abel. It was jealously that consumed Saul and overtook him.

Jealously is one of the key main temptations.

Why? If anger or wrath arises quickly you can choose to avoid any action and calm down.

But jealously takes meditation on selfishness, and meditation leads to actions. And those actions will eventually be devastating. And in the end, you will only do yourself more harm than you would care to bear.

If you have been jealous recently, go ahead and start anew by taking it to the altar of grace. If someone has been jealous of you, why not pray for that person now?

Tomorrow's lesson: How to never lack again...

Chapter 28 - Success Lesson #28: How to NEVER lack again

Today's power verse comes from **Verse 27 of Proverbs 28**:

"He that giveth unto the poor shall not lack: but he that hideth his eyes shall have many a curse".

The poor have a special place in the heart of God. So much so that when Jesus gave the disciples the commission, the first thing He said was to preach the Gospel to the poor.

What is the Good News to the poor? That God loves them.

He is with them. And if they would believe the Good News, He will deliver them. He is all they will ever need.

If they seek first the Kingdom of God (His way of doing and being right) then all things they need will be added unto them.

That is why crying and fasting about it won't change anything. We need to preach

the Good News to them. Emmanuel: God
with us!

When you give to the poor, according
to **Jeremiah 7, it is God who will repay
you**. What an incentive to do the work of
God!

You can't out give a king; how much more
will the King of Kings do for you for being
the instrument of blessing in someone's
life?

**God's ways are ways to bless you; not to
curse you. Because He loves you He is
giving you a key to not lack: give to the
poor.**

If you act as though the poor do not exist,
then what are you demonstrating through
your actions? How deep is your love for
God and humankind if the poor are of no
concern to you?

It doesn't mean to turn over your paycheck,
but it does mean to at least begin to think

of ways to be part of the solution.

If you never want to lack again, take God at
His Word; He will back it up.

Tomorrow's lesson: Why you need to
see...

**Chapter 29 - Success Lesson #29: You
need to see in order to live**

Today's power verse comes from **Verse 18
of Proverbs 29**:

*"Where [there is] no vision, the people
perish: but he that keepeth the law, happy
[is] he"*.

From the different translations of the Bible,
you can get a better understanding of this
verse.

The New American Standard Bible says
that the people are unrestrained.

The Amplified states that those who keep
the law are blessed, happy, fortunate, and
enviable.

The NLT states that people who do not
accept divine guidance run wild.

Let's define a vision. **A vision is defined as
a divine revelation.** It is a well-formed
goal. When you don't have a vision, you

can't perform. You can't perform because
you can't conceive it.

What can't be conceived cannot be born.
You will be defeated before you are in even
in a fight.

**The power of vision is utterly important
to success.** For example, the power of
vision is used many times in business.
They call it forecasting sales for the
following month. What is forecasting but a
well-defined goal?

Divine revelation will keep you on track in
spite of, the pit you are in; in spite any
bondage that might come upon you; in
spite of any lies that might be said of you.

Isn't that the lesson we learn from Joseph's
life?

So when we don't have divine revelation for
our lives, we end up unrestrained. We end
up running wild.

But when we receive divine revelation of
what to do, then we will be blessed, happy,
fortunate, and enviable. Receive your divine
revelation today and live!

Tomorrow's lesson: Be a coney..

Chapter 30: Success Lesson #30: Be a coney!

Today's power verse comes from **Verse 26 of Proverbs 30**:

"The conies are but feeble folk yet make their houses in the rocks"

Conies are a type of rabbit. They are found in the Middle East, Africa, and Asia.

In this series of teaching based on four animals, the coney represents how to avoid risk and loss by choosing the best protection.

The smallest of creatures can teach us something. Just look at how diligently the ant works for the future!

Locusts understand the power in numbers. The spider goes where most animals can't.

So what is the life of a coney to teach us?

The only defense this rabbit has is speed in retreating. May we be so wise when we are put in danger!

Most of the danger that comes to us is not life threatening, but in going along with something we know we shouldn't do.

Instead of running, we stand there thinking about it. Don't think about it. Run!

There are ways of safety that you can implement if you are feeble.

You might not know much about finances, but you can put money away in a mutual fund.

You might not know much about health, but you can visit the doctor for some instruction.

You might not know much about the Word of God, but you can continue to get lessons like this one that will help shed some light for you.

When you are in danger, run to the rock: Jesus. He is steadfast and guarantees your future when you put your trust in Him!

<u>Tomorrow's Lesson:</u> A Woman of Worth

Chapter 31 – Success Lesson # 31: A Woman of Worth

Last but not least, we've finally reached Chapter 31, the final chapter in Proverbs.

In my opinion, God saved the best chapter for last because it specifically talks about the characteristics of a Woman of Worth, a virtuous woman, if you will. There are so many keys that the make up a woman of worth in this chapter that I have broken down these keys into 10 separate virtues.

There are multiple power verses in today's lesson.

1. Verses 29-31 speak about Faith - A Virtuous Woman serves God with all of her heart, mind, and soul. She seeks His will for her life and follows His ways.

2. Verses 11,12 speak about Marriage – A Virtuous Woman respects her husband. She does him good all the days of her life. She is trustworthy and a helpmeet.

3. <u>Verse 28 talks about Mothering</u> - A Virtuous Woman teaches her children the ways of her Father in heaven. She nurtures her children with the love of Christ, disciplines them with care and wisdom, and trains them in the way they should go.

4. <u>Verses 14, 15 talk about Health</u> – A Virtuous Woman cares for her body. She prepares healthy food for her family.

5. <u>Verse 20 teaches about Service</u> - A Virtuous Woman serves her husband, her family, her friends, and her neighbors with a gentle and loving spirit. She is charitable.

6. <u>Verse 18 teaches about Finances</u> - A Virtuous Woman seeks her husband's approval before making purchases and spends money wisely. She is careful to purchase quality items her family needs.

7. <u>Verse 24 speaks about being Industrious</u> – A Virtuous Woman works willingly with her hands. She sings praises to God and does not grumble while completing her tasks.

8. Verse 27 talks about making a Home –
A Virtuous Woman is a homemaker.
She creates an inviting atmosphere of
warmth and love for her family and guests.
She uses hospitality to minister to those
around her.

**9. Verse 19 teaches about Time
management** - A Virtuous Woman uses her
time wisely. She works diligently to
complete her daily tasks. She does not
spend time dwelling on those things that do
not please the Lord.

**10. Verse 10 teaches about a Woman of
Worth and Beauty –** A Virtuous Woman is
a woman of worth and beauty. She has
the inner beauty that only comes from
Christ. She uses her creativity and sense of
style to create beauty in her life and the
lives of her loved ones.

As you can see, there are numerous virtues
that describe and define a woman of worth.

If you are a man and seeking a formidable
mate to help you build the proper home,
then these are the characteristics you
should seek in a woman.

If you are a woman, you already have these
virtues, thus, you should have someone in
your life that will allow you to continue to
exhibit these exceptional qualities.

By finding that special person that will allow
you to contribute those virtues, together
you will find unspeakable success and have
a union truly favored by God.

Chapter 32:   A Final Note

Final Note:

I hope you have enjoyed this book. I
challenge all of you to continue reading
Proverbs daily for one year and I promise
you the next year will be the best
ever **IF** you apply the principles learned.

According to the prologue (1:1-7), Proverbs
was written to give "prudence to the simple,
knowledge and discretion to the young"
(1:4), and to make the wise even wiser (1:5)

Whatever your desires and goals are for
success, you are now well on your way to
achieving the life you desire!

God Bless!!!

Scotty V. Jones

For more Proverbial Success
products, visit our website at
ProverbialSuccessOnline.com

If you are interested in other
books, coaching or other
products from Scotty V. Jones,
visit ScottyVJones.com